Thank you to Dave, Hillary, Lyle, and Darren AND to all the Smiley Captains.
I am grateful, every day, that you have given me so much to smile about.
—Ruth

Ruth Kaiser, an artist, a teacher, an author, and a mom, is the creator of the Spontaneous Smiley Project. In 2008, having seen smiley faces all her life, she began sharing her smiley photos on Facebook. Much to her surprise, people from all over the world began submitting their own smiley photos. What was once her own goofy little hobby has become a feel-good endeavor for people all over the world.

You can upload your own Spontaneous Smileys, and become a Smiley Captain, at SpontaneousSmiley.com.

Each uploaded photo generates a $1 donation to Operation Smile, which provides free surgeries for children born with facial deformities.

Spontaneous
Smiley

The Smiley Book of COLORS

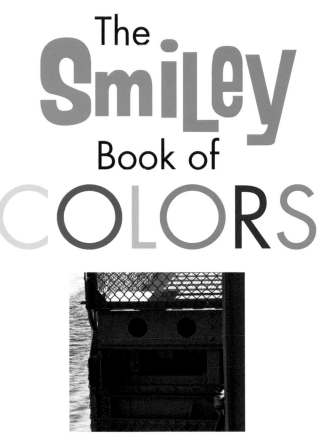

By Ruth Kaiser

A GOLDEN BOOK • NEW YORK

Text and photographs copyright © 2012 by Ruth Kaiser. All rights reserved.
Published in the United States by Golden Books, an imprint of Random House Children's Books,
a division of Random House, Inc., 1745 Broadway, New York, NY 10019. Golden Books,
A Golden Book, and the G colophon are registered trademarks of Random House, Inc.
www.randomhouse.com/kids
Educators and librarians, for a variety of teaching tools, visit us at
www.randomhouse.com/teachers
Library of Congress Control Number: 2011921186
ISBN: 978-0-375-86983-9 (trade)—ISBN: 978-0-375-96983-6 (lib. bdg.)
PRINTED IN CHINA
10 9 8 7 6 5 4 3 2 1
Random House Children's Books supports the First Amendment and celebrates the right to read.

Smile! Be happy!

It's contagious—
Like the good feeling you'll get
From these smiley-filled pages.

You'll find smileys
Wherever you turn. . . .

We've found that happiness
Is something you learn.

Decide to notice,
And smileys appear.
You'll giggle! You'll laugh!
You'll grin ear to ear!

ORANGE

Smile! Be happy!
You get to pick—
When something is icky,
Do you focus on ick?

YELLOW

Look all around
And notice the good!
Focus on that.

GREEN

CELL PHONES

INKJET CARTRIDGES

RECYCLE HERE!
THANK YOU

We think you should.

That's the idea!
Choose good instead.
Talk to yourself
With that voice in your head.

BLUE

Might all be okay?
Might it really be fine?
Tell yourself, "Yes!"
Life is *yours* to define!

PURPLE

A problem seems small
When you cut it some slack.

PINK

You can choose to forgive

And how you react.

In every moment,
All the day through:
Smile or frown?

GRAY

It's up to you.

Smile! Be happy!
It's a choice you can choose.
Give it a try—
You've got nothing to lose!

BLACK

Here is the lesson
That we want to share:
There's a happier life

You can pull from thin air.

Smile! Be happy
In this beautiful place—
Made more so each day
By the smile on *your* face!

BROWN

Ski Smiley

Skirt Smiley

Car Smiley

Fishy Leaf Smiley

Persimmons Smiley

Cake Smiley

Doctor's Tape Smiley

Wagon Handle Smile

Shopping Cart Smiley

Car Door Smiley

Taillight Smiley

Stapler Smiley

Shoe Smiley

Straw & Wheels Smiley

House Smiley

Toy Truck Smiley